Dearest of Captains

Captain Sally Louisa Tompkns, C.S.A.

Photograph courtesy of the
Eleanor S. Brockenbrough Library
The Museum of the Confederacy, Richmond, Virginia.

Dearest of Captains

A biography of
Sally Louisa Tompkins

Keppel Hagerman

BRANDYLANE PUBLISHERS
White Stone, Virginia 22578

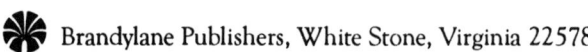 Brandylane Publishers, White Stone, Virginia 22578

Copyright 1996 by Keppel Hagerman.
All rights reserved. Published 1996.
Printed in the United States of America.

Back cover photograph courtesy of the Eleanor S. Brockenbrough Library,
The Museum of the Confederacy, Richmond, Virginia.

Library of Congress Cataloging-in-Publication Data

Hagerman, Keppel, 1919-
    Dearest of captains: a biography of Sally Louisa Tompkins/Keppel Hagerman.
    p. cm.
  ISBN 1-883911-09-05
    1. Tompkins, Sally Louisa, 1833-1916—Poetry. 2. Hospitals, Voluntary—Virginia—Richmond—History—19th century—Poetry.
3. United States—History—Civil War, 1861-1865—Hospitals—Poetry.
4. United States—History—Civil War, 1861-1865—Women—Poetry.
5. Confederate States of America—Poetry.   I. Title.
PS3558.A32335D43   1996
811'.54—dc20   96-2696
                                                                CIP

For the Captains—

To the memory of my Confederate grandfather,
Captain J.A.M. Gwaltney
Troop B, First Cavalry, Virginia Volunteers
and
To my husband,
Captain George M. Hagerman, U.S. Navy (Ret.)

CONTENTS

Preface		page viii
Acknowledgments		page ix
Part I	Poplar Grove—1833-1849	page 1
Part II	The War—1861-1865	page 19
Part III	Richmond—1865-1916	page 61

PREFACE

This narrative poem is the story of Sally Louisa Tompkins, the only woman to be commissioned an officer in either the Army of the Confederacy or the Union Army.

Captain Sally was born at Poplar Grove in Mathews County, Virginia, November 9, 1833. From early childhood she showed a great love and aptitude for nursing.

Following the First Battle of Manassas she established her own private hospital in Richmond. Later in 1861 private hospitals were no longer able to draw medical supplies from the government, and were forced to close. Because of its excellent reputation for cleanliness and high recovery rates President Jefferson Davis commissioned Sally a Captain in the Confederate Cavalry, thus enabling her to draw government supplies and continue operating her Robertson's Hospital, which had the highest recovery rate of any military hospital, North or South.

Captain Sally died in Richmond, Virginia, July 25, 1916. This sequence of poems is her story, as I see it.

                                Keppel Hagerman
                                Charlottesville, Virginia

ACKNOWLEDGMENTS

I would like to acknowledge with much gratitude the help and support of Sybil Bazuin, historian and archivist for the Mathews County Historical Society, Mathews, Virginia; her generosity in making all papers pertaining to Sally Louisa Tompkins available to me.

Many thanks also to Dalton Mallory of Colonial Beach, Virginia for sharing his beautifully researched collection of the letters of Sally Tompkins.

Much appreciation to librarians who were patient and generous with their time and talents: Mrs. Martha Story of the Mathews Memorial Library, Mathews, Virginia, and Ms. Jackie Hite and Ms. Leslie Smail of the Post Library of Fort Story at Virginia Beach, Virginia.

Special thanks to St. James's Episcopal Church in Richmond, Virginia for permission to reproduce the stained glass window dedicated to the memory of Captain Sally Louisa Tompkins.

With affection and gratitude I wish to acknowledge the help of two splendid poets and teachers: Judy Goldman of Charlotte, North Carolina who critiqued the first draft of my manuscript; and Davis Milton McCombs, editorial assistant for *Poetry* magazine, whose insight and help were invaluable for my final revision of *Dearest of Captains*.

Finally to Robert H. Pruett, publisher of Brandylane Publishers and to his associate editor, Suzanne Best, thanks for their help and their encouragement.

> Keppel Hagerman
> Charlottesville, Virginia
> September 1995

Poplar Grove—1833-1849

Poplar Grove in 1984.

Photograph courtesy of Tidewater Newspapers, Inc.

The Poplar Grove Mill in Mathews County, Virginia.

Photograph courtesy of
The Mathews County Historical Society.

I. THE TIDE MILL AT POPLAR GROVE

Where reeds and marsh grass angle low
the mill wheels groan, powered
by the pull of lunar tides
that surge the sluice
from Chesapeake Bay.

Geese honk above the mill in autumn flight,
oblivious to the rumble of the stones
that grind the grain,
the creak of carts that trundle it
to Yorktown's war.

Clouds cast shadows on the river bed,
one conflict ends, another starts,
which like the tide
fragments the land.

Now a girl born close by the turning wheel
is destined, in the coming war, to heal.

II. POPLAR GROVE

The house sprawls across the hill,
slopes to the edge of East River
within sight of the tide mill.
White-columned, a gentleman farmer's home
with wings added as the family grows.

Built by Colonel Thomas Patterson,
it is a river house
of bird calls and wild things,
pheasant, deer, rabbits,
fish spawned in tidal waters.

A serpentine wall of brick,
Tom Jefferson's design,
circles the garden, flanked by oak, magnolia,
towering poplars, stately symbols of the Whigs.

Behind the big house
squat quarters for the Colonel's slaves,
who run the mill, farm the land,
provide house servants for the family.
They pull boots on and off, button gentlemens' shirts,
tie daughters' sashes, brush flaxen curls.

Below they cook and serve
wild game, crabs from the bay:
daily dust the mahogany sideboard,
while lame Joe buffs the Colonel's English silver,
chants softly:
"Go down, Moses, way down in Egypt land."

III. PHOEBE PONDERS

Miz Tompkins tell me
she going to have one more.
I'se tired of tending babies,
but I can't say no to Missus.

Turn out to be a baby girl,
they names her Sally Louisa.
She not like the others—
that chile got plenty smarts.

She ain't got no mind for books,
stays outside all day.
She ain't going to be much to look at—
holds her mouth too firm.

She goes out to our cabins
to comfort the sick and old,
she search the woods for ailing critters,
don't mind being all alone.

I loves this chile, her diff'rent ways,
she be both smart and good.
When Miss Sally grows up, she sure 'nuff
going to amount to something.

IV. SALLY'S FAMILY

Papa has four children from another wife
when he marries Mama,
then four more with Mama;
two sisters and a brother are mine, I'm the baby.
Phoebe says I am the smallest and smartest,
but not to tell the others.
Grandpa Patterson fought with George Washington,
built Poplar Grove where Mama was born.
I live here with seven siblings.
Papa is rich, and Mama loves parties,
so do my sisters and brothers.
Elizabeth and I sit on the stairs,
peep down at the dancers,
watch them whirl through the Virginia reel.
Mama glistens in black silk,
sisters Martha and Maria in rose and blue,
brothers handsome in ruffled waistcoats.
Mrs. Wiggle plays harpsichord,
while Jeremiah fiddles.
Finally I start to nod,
then Lizzie takes me to her room.
From her big bed I watch the moon
fill the river with light.

V. SALLY'S WORK

Mama calls me again to come in;
if she only knew
how much I have to do out here.
I can't leave before I make a splint
for the bluebird with a broken wing.
It's always Mama or Phoebe or Brother Ben
wanting me to wash or study or have tea.
Only Lizzie understands
that what I love
is caring for the hurt animals,
the birds and newborn kittens—
they need me.

SALLY'S SONG

Here birds serenade in spring,
when poplar trees turn green.
I wander through the woods and sing;
here birds serenade in spring.
To the woods I like to bring
myself alone, and sit and dream,
hear birds serenade in spring,
when poplar trees turn green.

VI. LIZZIE'S MEDITATION

Now Sister Sally sleeps,
a small bundle in the big bed
we've shared since she was born,
and I was seventeen. We loved each other
from the start; she's followed me
in devotion to God's word.
While I braid her hair, I tell her
Bible tales; she knows them by heart.
I love my other sisters—so caught up
in housekeeping, quilting bees, babies,
but I don't covet their lives.

I lean from the window,
hear the silky lapping of river waves.
The moon has floated out of sight,
the stars are pale and far away.
One tumbles from the sky,
a sign that someone I know will die.

Moon, so high in the heavens,
you must touch God.
Stars, old as time, you are wise.
Send me an answer
to my quest for Him.

VII. LIZZIE'S TASK

Through prayer it came to her
to rebuild Kingston Parish Church,
for twenty years in ruins.
First she spent her own inheritance.
The family aided fragile Lizzie,
ate butter only on Sunday,
gathered flower and vegetable seeds
to sell to Norfolk merchants,
also healing salves concocted with Sally's help,
then packed in boxes made by brother Ben
from boxwood in the garden.

Vehemently she refused loans from uncles;
abandoned her retiring, timid ways,
and alone sought donations, workmen, and materials
throughout the parish.
In a year Christ Church rose again
due to Lizzie's dedication.
Only nine months were left for her to live
after accomplishing her mission.

LIZZIE'S EPILOGUE—SEPTEMBER 2, 1842

Sally child, don't weep for me,
my work on earth is done.
Though young, you have the gift of healing,
I know you, too, will serve;
and we'll be reunited in God's hereafter.

VIII. AT THE QUARTERS

Mama says I may go
with Phoebe to the quarters.
Cook gives us tea, biscuits, sorghum
for the field hands stricken with fever.
Each morning Uncle Solomon brings the sick
to Papa's old office where
Mama comforts them.
So much work for Mama since Papa died,
even with Brother Benjamin's help.
She says it's her duty,
but I don't think she loves being there
like I do.

In the quarters Uncle puts beads around his neck,
a charm to make folks well.
Phoebe tells me not to go in the back
where six-year-old Jasper may have the pox.
While Phoebe hands around food,
I walk with Uncle and Aunt Sylvie, his helper;
she tells me who is ill
and what is wrong.
John's eyes have running sores.
Jelly made from sassafras soaked in water
seems to ease the pain.
Since Prissy's new baby died, she moans and wails
and wilts with fever.
Aunt Sylvie says she'll die too.

I ask Aunt Sylvie why they
can't let blood, or use leeches
like when Papa was ill.
She says only a real white man doctor
can do that, it's never done to colored folks.
Old Homer got a snake bite,
Uncle says Homer's lucky he's not dead,
gives me rags dipped in turpentine and wild indigo,
lets me stroke the wound.
"You mighty kind, little Missy," Homer whispers.
Phoebe comes running.
"Homer, you old fool, this chile ain't supposed
to touch you sick folk.
Miss Sally, I'm going to take you home."

IX. SALLY GROWN UP

At sunset I stroll down
to the river's edge
to be alone,
listen to the creak of the tide mill.
At 17, my time of month
has only just started.
I tell Phoebe,
as Mama is so worried these days.
Today down in the quarters,
I listen to old Uncle Solomon
talk about his cures for ailments.
I'd love to be a doctor,
know that's impossible.
I think hard about how I can best do
what I want—
I commune in prayer with Lizzie.

There's talk of war coming
between the North and the South.
Last week Mr. Calvert from Maryland
visited my half-brothers:
I heard them late into the night.
Even at breakfast,
usually a jolly time at Poplar Grove,
everyone was solemn.

A flock of bluebirds
swoops over the wall,
and is gone;
black ravens fill the space.

I hear Phoebe calling me for dinner.
The mill always sounds the same,
belts flapping and slapping.
The rumbling comforts me.
If war comes, I wonder what will happen to the mill,
what will happen to us.
Phoebe calls again.
I stare at the ravens winging across the river,
run up the hill through the wide white doors
to dinner.

X. FAREWELL TO POPLAR GROVE 1849

Now that Brother Ben is gone,
it's decided that we women-folk
should move to Norfolk—
it's too much for Mama.
She tries to be brave,
but she goes through each room,
weeping, saying good-bye.
I know its selfish,
but I'm not too sad,
think I might have a chance
to do what I want
in some other place.

Late afternoon, we're packed at last,
Mama, Sister Maria, Phoebe and me;
other servants will follow.
I turn in the carriage,
look hard once more at Poplar Grove,
but mists from the river
cover the mill, conceal the house.
All that's left to see are the quarters,
dark against the twilight,
thin smoke rising from one.
I hear a baby's cry.

I ask Mama to stop a minute at Christ Church
so I can put a flower on Lizzie's grave.
I remember her promise that
we'll meet again.

And now Churchill cracks the whip,
we commence the first lap of our journey;
tonight Auburn on the North River,
where Sister Martha lives.
Tomorrow we'll sail with the tides
in Brother Ben's packet "Belvedera,"
for Norfolk, where Maria and I will attend
the Norfolk Female Institute.

Phoebe knows how I loved Poplar Grove,
the quarters, the animals, and the river.
But, like me, she knows it's time to leave.

XI. SALLY'S MOTHER REFLECTS

Confined with painful pleurisy,
my ribs constrict.
Out the window
my school-bound daughters are led
by faithful Phoebe, broad as the pathway,
her head tied in a red kerchief.

Placid Maria does not concern me,
but Sally has a restless nature.
Always eager to study plagues and agues,
she reads every line in the "THE NORFOLK VIRGINIAN,"
about foreign seamen smitten
with a deadly epidemic.

My husband's solicitors, the Taylors,
protect us, advise caution in the streets
that swarm with strangers—
British, Dutch, and French sailors.

Both girls are diligent in school,
Sally excels in Biblical history.
I believe her love of nursing is
more Biblical than medical.
Lately when I'm ailing she watches me
with her night-dark eyes.
I don't doubt her love for me,
but know she's curious about my symptoms, too.

Soon I must decide where we should live.
I think our future is in Richmond,
home of close relations,
and more traditional than this noisy seaport.

Poplar Grove is sold,
I, a widow with two children dead,
two to raise,
am a ball of yarn unravelling.

The War—1861-1865

The Robertson Hospital in Richmond, Virginia.
Photograph courtesy of
The Mathews County Historical Society.

"In May 1861 it was decided to transfer the capital of the Confederacy from Montgomery, Alabama to Richmond, Virginia, because of Virginia's prestige, a move which, considering Richmond's proximity to the North, has generally been regarded as a serious mistake."

                Article, THE CONFEDERACY
                COLUMBIA ENCYCLOPEDIA
                Volume III

I. AT ARLINGTON HOUSE 1861

Here in this overcrowded hotel
at dinner time we are a Tower of Babel,
so many different accents
it's hard to recognize a Virginian.
Everyone talks at once
in high-pitched tones, and fast
as firecrackers.
Maria can tell who's from Alabama,
or North or South Carolina.
Last night a Frenchman, M. Picard,
(it's whispered he sells guns)
spoke of "his husband" and "two childs,"
back home in France.
Maria and I could barely control our laughter.

All talk is of the coming conflict,
and Richmond chosen for the seat of government;
some say, unwisely.
It's been called a stuck-up city;
I think it's beautiful.
high on seven hills like Rome
above the rust-colored James River.

Here Papa had friends in high places.
He said Richmond was rich
from tobacco trade
and selling slaves—
such wicked ways to wealth.
We have nice cousins here.
For now there's nowhere else in all the world
I'd rather be.

II. REVERIE AT ST. JAMES'S, June 1861

After services Maria and Cousin Emmie
leave the church;
I stay behind to think and pray.
Pastor's sermon was somber today—
the war, the war, the war,
and the suffering it will bring.
Now in this stillness,
light reflects from the jewelled windows.
Oh, God, I've prayed to know
what I should do in this coming war.
Show me some special way
to use my small talents.
Lizzie, I need you.

These sacred windows strengthen me.
The white is my faith, purple is Christ,
the red is His blood—
I'm overcome with grief
when I think about the blood.
In this quiet place I'm guided
how best to serve my Lord.

Now I'll rejoin Maria and Emmie
and enjoy the bright summer day;
we'll ask Belle Stuart to accompany us
to Pazzini's for Italian ices.

July 21, 1861-MANASSAS

"The victory at Bull Run though decisive and important in both its moral and physical effects had been dearly bought. Altogether the Confederates estimated their casualties in dead and wounded just under 1,900; of that number approximately 500 were killed."

>   *JEFFERSON DAVIS,*
>   *CONFEDERATE PRESIDENT*
>   Volume I
>   Hudson Strode.

III. AFTER MANASSAS

Now Richmond is
like *A Tale of Two Cities*,
when tumbrels carried the condemned to guillotine.
Here carts lumber through the streets
with the mutilated, the wounded
screaming "Mother," "Help me, Christ."
The vans provided by the Southern Express Co.
are all stained scarlet now.
No preparations have been made for such carnage.
The newly built almshouse
becomes Hospital Number One.
tobacco warehouses fill with cots,
pleas for help go out to private homes.
Medicine, blankets, bandages, nurses
are all in short supply.

My prayers are answered by God
and Papa's old friend Judge Robertson,
whose family has fled to a remote farm
for the war's duration.
He tendered me keys to his residence
on Third and Main Streets, close to the James.
I am drawn to rivers,
soothing with their sibilant murmur,
unchanged beneath the noise of Richmond.

I've purchased supplies
with my inheritance.
Mammy Phoebe, Mama's cook, and one other
preside in the kitchen.

My Richmond friends serve as nurses.
Belle Stuart laughed today telling
how she offered to bathe the face
of a young infantryman from Tennessee;
"You can if you want to, Ma'am, it don't need it,
fourteen ladies have already had the pleasure."

IV. SALLY'S ORDEAL

Two days ago the orders came that
all private hospitals must close forthwith.
I'm prostrate with disbelief and grief.
Excessive malingering,
the recovered still feigning illness,
great numbers don't return to duty,
are the reasons given for this order.
Now it seems government hospitals
multiply like chickweed.
Chimborazo expands,
new hospitals at Camp Jackson, Camp Winder,
and Howard Grove.
All has gone well here,
our recovery figures are high.
I keep detailed account
of the number of boys returned
to their commands,
greater then any hospital in Richmond.

I must solve this problem, and quickly.
TRUST IN THE LORD WITH ALL THINE HEART,
HE SHALL DIRECT THY PATHS.
I'm guided to implore Papa's kinsman
Judge William Crump, now Assistant Secretary of Treasury
to arrange a meeting with Mr. Jefferson Davis.
YEA, THOU ART MY ROCK AND MY FORTRESS,
FOR THY NAME'S SAKE, LEAD ME AND GUIDE ME.

All through the night
I delve deep into the scriptures.
GOD IS OUR REFUGE AND STRENGTH
A VERY PRESENT HELP IN TROUBLE.
Tomorrow I meet with the President.
I shall meditate and pray until daybreak.
FINALLY MY BRETHREN, BE STRONG IN THE LORD,
AND IN THE POWER OF HIS MIGHT.

V. JUDGE WILLIAM CRUMP RECORDS THE EVENTS OF SEPTEMBER 9, 1861

At nine o'clock I call for Miss Sally.
Her maidservant Phoebe places
two books in her hands,
a prayer book and what looks like a records book.
My kinswoman is pale this morning,
shadows under her dark eyes,
black hair in tight braids.
She is dressed in black from her boots
to a small bonnet tied under her chin.
There's a determined look
to her eyes and mouth
that reminds me of her grandpa Colonel Patterson.
For certain, she's no beauty,
grim and prim I'd call her.
She assures me that she's quite well.
I've been told she is pious and straight-laced,
and that, true to her military heritage,
she runs her hospital like a Prussian drill master.

We drive through the oven heat of September
to the family entrance
of the gleaming White House of the Confederacy
where a tall black footman announces our arrival.
The President appears—tall, fair, dignified, remote.
The parlor is smartly embellished
with velvet draperies, a plum-colored carpet,
the fireplace flanked by two fine Belter rosewood consoles.

I am thankful that today Mr. Davis
seems free of the neuralgia which frequently torments him.
He is a handsome man, eyes blue as tempered steel;
if only he could unbend a little.
He tells Miss Sally in his melodious voice
that he's aware she receives no pay;
has financed Robertson's Hospital herself.
He's mindful of its reputation
for exacting cleanliness.
In a firm voice she speaks
of the high standards she demands.
Pacing the floor, he replies
he cannot ignore government regulations.

She places before him the hospital register,
points out the neat columns
of rank, name, company, regiment of each patient;
date admitted, malady, and date of cure.
There's no denying that Mr. Davis is impressed;
and so am I.
For an interminable moment he pauses,
stares out the window
at a large magnolia.
Miss Sally doesn't flinch, her lips move
as if in prayer.
I hear the breathing of the three of us in the stifling heat.
Then uncharacteristically, the President smiles:
"Miss Tompkins we will make you an officer
in the Army of the Confederacy.
You'll be under government jurisdiction,
and thus your hospital can be saved."

Sally's stern young face relaxes;
smiling, she grasps his hands.
Thereupon a secretary is called
to issue proper papers.
After thank-yous and good-byes,
the young woman who entered the White House
as Miss Tompkins
departs, commissioned Captain Sally Louisa Tompkins,
Confederate Cavalry.

VI. SALLY'S STAFF—September 10, 1861

I wake up this morning a captain,
God's solution to my problem.
I don't care about the captain part,
the government pay—I won't accept it.
My joy is that our hospital continues.
This morning I'll summon my staff
to share the great news.
From the window, I listen
to the river gurgling below;
I can always hear it, no matter
how noisy it is inside.

Dr. Garnett, our head surgeon, tells me
my rank is the same as assistant surgeon.
A sturdy man, late of Washington,
he gave up a growing practice
to return to his native state; war disrupts us all.
Unflappable under stress,
he, like me, despairs of needless amputations.
Six young doctors assist him.
He refuses to accept a cent from government.

My faithful helpers share my joy—
Phoebe, my beloved Mammy,
and also from Poplar Grove, the two Betsys.
The men delight in calling smiling Betsy
"Sad Betsy," the more lugubrious one "Glad Betsy."
Glad or sad, they labor long hours
at grim and dirty work, assisted by one steward.

John Crumley, our Irish gardener
grows miracles behind the hospital that he in turn
surrenders to chief cook Sallie.
His hands, as skilled in his profession,
as those of our surgeons,
encourage strength and healing.
Giant eggplant, tomatoes, onions,
like gifts of healthy organs,
nourish ailing men.

"With the men at war the women of the Confederacy, those supposedly frail, delicate creatures of the Southern chivalric legend, bravely carried on at home supporting the cause as best they could. They did not face wholesale death as did the soldiers in the field, yet they knew war as it was brought to them in the mighty Union invasion of 1864-65."

                    Article, THE CONFEDERACY
                    COLUMBIA ENCYCLOPEDIA,
                    Volume III

VII. LADIES OF THE ROBERTSON HOSPITAL

Like clouds of butterflies they swoop and dart,
vivid against whitewashed walls.
Bearing gifts of flowers, fruits,
Italian confections from Pazzini's,
they chatter, laugh and banter
with the convalescents.
Rosy girls come with mammies,
maids and butlers accompany the matrons,
alternate vigils by night and day.
They bandage wounds, fan off flies, fetch water,
search for non-existent ice.
In their gardens they cultivate poppies
for a few drops of tincture of opium.
Richmond belles who dance all night,
by day turn into nurses.
An elder lady, eyes tight with sorrow,
two sons and a husband fighting the war,
goes off in a huff at a burly countryman's remark
that she's a spry old lark,
but she returns next day to his bedside.

I watch my boys
tormented by hopeless yearning
for Susanna with her great black eyes,
Nancy of the auburn curls, all the soft hands
and breasts trembling over the beds.

I admire their courage
in the face of public criticism, male resentment.
Still I think it would be good
if the ladies could leave their beauty at the door,
bring in only their goodness and energy.

VIII. CORPORAL JENKINS SENDS A LETTER HOME

Dear Ma,
After them long weeks of bullets and beans,
I'm sure eating good. Instead of hard tack, it's
jellies and custards, chicken and stews;
and I'm resting in a clean bed too.

There's a powerful lot of scrubbing and washing here,
my beard is done shaved, my hair cut neat,
and clean drawers every morning.
I ain't been this pure since the day I was born.

At bedtime Miss Sally calls us to kneel,
even though some got to handle a crutch,
We call her "the little lady
with the milk white hands."
Ma, you'd be glad the way
she prays and reads us the Word.
                Your loving son,
                Abner Jenkins, Jr.

IX. DR. GARNETT REFLECTS

My captain's rounds begin at dawn.
As if prodded by invisible spurs,
she flits from bed to bed,
Bible in hand, medicine kit
strapped to her side.
In no way do the men intend mockery,
when they joke about her reticule
which contains the keys
to unlock precious laudanum and brandy.

This morning we received a visitor,
the celebrated Mrs. Mary Chestnut of South Carolina,
who, it's rumored, possesses
a sharp eye and a quick tongue.
She sailed in rather grandly, accompanied by a maid.
On meeting Captain Sally she asked:
"Are there any Carolinians here?"
My captain's instant reply:
"I never ask where the sick and wounded come from."

Not a day goes by that
Miss Sally isn't tendered a proposal of marriage.
No coy bones in this lady's body, she replies,
"Lad, you must still be sick of your fevers."
When returned to duty, she gives
each man a blanket roll
wrapped in oilcloth, filled with
clean clothes, a prayer book and the Gospels.
Together they pray, then she sends him back to war.

X. CORPORAL JENKINS HAS A NIGHT OUT

I done got permission
to stroll out to town.
Had me a whore and a quart of good whiskey.
When I finally found my way back
to Robertson's
that little lady done jumped on me.
Then she made me kneel and pray,
plumb took all my clothes away.
This morning I had me
a hell of a headache.
My clothes locked up, I stayed in bed.
I asked the Captain's pardon—that lady ranks me.

XI. SALLY VISITS CHIMBOROZO HOSPITAL

Tonight I am in need of a river,
the brackish smell of marsh grass,
willows reflected in water,
birds skimming the surface, the splash of fish.
I want to lay my head on Phoebe's bosom,
ask her to take me home to Poplar Grove,
where the clatter of the tide mill
would help me forget what I saw today—
wooden legs tapping the corridors,
so many amputations, stumps of arms and legs,
some still oozing,
spreading the deadly pyemia and effluvia.

In my register by each man's name,
I note the nature of his malady—
malaria, typhoid fever, whooping cough.
The wounds from minie balls
to hips, necks, eyes are
raw, ragged, red—better red than green.
My supplies dwindle to whisky, hoarhound, turpentine.
I will not use government issues
of poisonous lead, arsenic, mercury.
We urgently need chloroform, morphine, quinine.

After prayers I'll try to sleep,
soothed by the lapping of the James
two streets below.
Tomorrow I will search for a blockade runner.

XII. DEAREST OF CAPTAINS

Word reaches me I'm wanted at Robertson's Hospital
to discuss procurement of medical supplies.
I'm told there's a lady in charge.
I, Anthony Snowden, blockade runner for this Southern cause,
formerly an officer in Her Majesty's Navy
with a questionable discharge,
dress with care, apply a bit of brilliantine
in the French manner to my hair.
Since I will see a lady, I contemplate
a pleasant dalliance.
So far no success with the Richmond belles—
so intense in their dedication
to the Cause, they have no heart
for flirting with an Englishman.
They have eyes only for their boys in butternut and gray—
poor gallant devils, who won't survive
Yankee industrialization.
I have a special fondness for gallantry,
and for captaining my sleek ship SOUTHERN CROSS,
which lies low in the water; she can out-maneuver
the fastest Federal man-o-war.
I can't deny this is profitable sport for me.

At the appointed hour I arrive at Robertson's.
A large Negro woman bids me enter;
soon thereafter a small lass dressed in black
appears, announces herself as Captain Sally Tompkins,
Confederate Cavalry.
My eyes rivet to her spare frame,
reticule strapped at her waist,
to the pale skin of her face and hands.

There's no frivolity here,
nor beauty except in the intensity of her expression,
As she explains her needs in a sombre voice,
my thoughts of romantic play vanish;
instead I'm charmed by her earnest conversation.
When she offers to show me around I follow gladly.

By God, I've never seen a cleaner house,
nor noted deeper respect than
from these ailing men.
On her part it's total dedication
to her Confederates.
When we return to her office,
she extends her hand and says:
"Can you help me, Captain Snowden?"
I bend low to kiss her hand, proclaim her
"Dearest of Captains," promise her all she wishes,
within my power to procure.
I banish the thought I'd have had her in bed,
(for that she'd have no aptitude nor interest.)
Dearest of Captains, I salute your integrity instead.

XIII. SUNDAY DINNER, July 22, 1862

Dear Cousin Mary:
I send this by Churchill our coachman
who leaves tomorrow for Gloucester
in search of food;
our rations grow slimmer, and so do we.
I have little time for letters—
there's much more to nursing
than caring for the sick.

Yesterday at St. Paul's church
I attended divine services with Cousin Emmie Crump.
We had just assembled
when a trooper clanked up the aisle,
thrust a paper into the hands of Reverend Minnegerode,
who blanched in the pulpit, as he read aloud
to the trembling congregation
a request for all citizens' aid
in feeding hungry men.
Veterans of the Valley campaign
would stop in Richmond for two hours
en route to further mayhem
somewhere east of the city.

Pastor asked each of us present
to leave church at once,
to prepare what food we had
for our gallant boys,
subsisting these past two months
on half rations.
At Robertson's I explained
the situation to patients and staff.

All agreed to forgo the special Sunday food
Cook Sallie had prepared,
(chicken, rice and a dozen just-baked apple pies)
for rations of fat bacon, Indian peas
with sorghum syrup on corn bread for dessert.

John Crumley hitched the wagon
and off we went.
Such a sight in Richmond's streets,
a strange procession of old men, children,
officers in uniform,
ladies in Sunday attire covered with aprons.
I spied Dr. Luke Meriweather, professor of Greek,
carrying a pan of bacon and cabbage,
a string of young girls holding trays of corn pone,
pitchers of sorghum, vinegar and water,
which we call "Confederate lemonade."

When we reached the line of freight and stock cars,
we wept over the dirty, ragged men,
many suffering with fevers and wounds.
Mothers found sons, sisters searched for brothers;
some looked in vain for loved ones.
The soldiers joked and cheered,
the women hid their tears.

After dispensing our vittles, we approached a medic
to offer the one bed available now at Robertson's.
He led us to a lad barely out of childhood,
ill and feverish—his name Nathan Newton,
a drummer boy, 12th Cavalry, Alabama Volunteers.

I sat in back with the delirious youth,
cradled his wounded head in my arms;
he could have been my son.
At Robertson's they are all my sons.
John Crumley drove us home
through the sad, silent streets of Richmond.
Pray for this boy, Mary, pray for me,
as I do for thee.
                              Your loving cousin,
                                   Sally

XIV. PHOEBE'S LAMENTATIONS

Miss Sally asked me to wash this chile,
who died befo' he had a life.
At fifteen he too young
for fightin' in this war.

His name Nathan Newton,
little boy from Birmingham.
For six weeks he linger on
callin' for his family.

He jus' a lamb of Jesus,
shouldn't never been no soldier.
I fold his pretty colored shirts
his Ma must have sewn.

I dress him in his gray suit,
combs his yellow hair.
Soon he be returning to his ma
in a sealed-up wooden box.

I almost finish packin'
feelin' mighty sad;
my heart 'bout nigh burst open
when I find his bright red drum.

I ain't never known my family,
most times lived with whites.
They been good to me,
Miss Sally like my own chile.

I've tried to soothe Sad Betsy,
she crying all the day.
She done heard that
her baby brother run off.

I hear tell of black men
fightin' one another;
don't make sense to free no slaves
who kills their own kind.

Oh, this war's
a low down misery
to black folks and to whites.

XV. SALLY TAKES INVENTORY—Autumn 1863

I hear Glad Betsy wailing,
"Nobody knows de trouble I've had,
nobody knows but Jesus."
This morning Cook reports an empty larder.
One bushel meal, a hundred dollars,
a barrel of flour, five hundred;
already we drink coffee made of wheat.
I've sent Churchill and John Crumley to Gloucester
in search of meat, apples, autumn vegetables.
They report the only food is fish from the Bay,
which we cannot preserve;
also the news that the Tide Mill is burned.
Those damned, damned Yankees.

Glad Betsy and I go to market every day,
return with empty baskets—there'll be no Christmas treats.
On my way this morning I meet Mrs. Carter Augustine,
who rambles at length (taking my time and her energy)
about new shoes for sale at one hundred fifty dollars;
the dilapidated state of our public buildings;
the influx of unwanted refugees to Richmond;
and the death of our beloved Stonewall.
Her tears flow, and I repress mine.
(Indeed she's right, his death a terrible loss for THE CAUSE.)

Finally the poor dear sails away,
with head held high, a real accomplishment
considering her enormous bonnet of green velvet
adorned with taffeta bow and trailing peacock feathers
in the style of ten years past.

Well, I'm no fashion plate, day after day
in black attire, covered by my nurse's apron.
I'm quite worn out and believe
meeting Mrs. Augustine has only added to my depression.
It's hard to stay cheerful, even for my boys,
with the war news so bad.

At Robertson's we're in great need
of quinine at one hundred eighty-eight dollars an ounce.
Each day the Betsy's seek
partridge berries, jimson weed, dandelion for tonics;
sumac provides a gurgle, wild ginger a stimulant;
I've found Indian turnip a powerful expectorant.
My Richmond ladies strip their homes of cotton
for dressing wounds.
I hear at Antietam corn leaves were used
as bandages by Clara Barton,
who stirred cauldrons of stew,
and ministered to the ill and dying.
Though she's a Yankee, I'd like to speak with her
of nursing. Well, stuff and nonsense, that's impossible.

XIV. CAPTAIN TOMPKINS RECORDS THE LAST LETTER OF LIEUTENANT PHILLIPPE BROUSSARD, AGE 21, 7TH INFANTRY, LOUISIANA REGULARS.

Sally

September 1863—
after Gettysburg

Of all my chores the saddest duty
is writing farewell letters for my lads
who'll not go home again.

◆ ◆ ◆ ◆ ◆

Phillippe

Dear Mother, Father, darling bride,
I feel my strength leaving,
but I need to share these final thoughts.
Missy, sweetheart, through sheets of pain
I search for your dear body,
now forever lost to me.
So precious has life been
I don't want to let it go.
How does my dying make us free?

If you should ask how I died,
and are told "at peace,"
it would be a monstrous lie.
For the beloved South I fought,
lost two legs and my good sight.
Now I question why, why?
I cannot help but despise
what causes such maddening pain.
Christ, what's all the killing for?

♦ ♦ ♦ ♦ ♦

Sally

I regret to write Phillippe died protesting violently,
not peacefully. His last words were:
"Mama, Papa, Missy, weep, weep for me."

XVII. ANOTHER REVERIE AT ST. JAMES'S—
WINTER 1864

So long ago it seems
I sat here filled with hope.
Now at twilight I remember
the first fresh days at Robertson's.
This war winds down, but not the dying.
The wounded lie unattended on railway platforms;
in Hollywood Cemetery, day after day
the mounds increase;
bodies interred without clothing, shoes or prayers.
I try to seal my ears
to words that rattle loosely everywhere:
submission, surrender,
subjugate, evacuate,
reconstruction.

In the dying sun, stained glass
washes me with colors;
the purple, Christ,
white, my faith.
But now it seems there's too much red.
It threatens to obscure everything else.

XVIII. CAPTAIN SALLY WATCHES THE FIRES
APRIL 2-3, 1865

Wagons, carts, carriages
thunder through the streets
leaving this doomed town.
The sweet sour smell of whiskey,
barrels emptied in the gutters,
sickens the air.
And now the shrieks of freed Negroes,
"Jesus has opened the way!"
mix with the drunken cries of men
escaped from jail.

The most terrible sound of all—
flames crackling
along the tobacco warehouses,
the acrid smell of the weed.
Shells exploding at the arsenal
compete with shouts from the streets,
"The Yankees are coming!"
I hear the sounds of their horses,
outbursts of martial music,
"Yankee Doodle," "John Brown's Body."
From the window I see the Federal flag
where only yesterday flew our proud stars and bars.
I see Negroes embrace the knees
of the invaders' horses.

Our government's fled to Danville.
The Yankees our only hope for law and order?
I vow I'll never seek their help.

Five streets west of us,
the fires sweep toward the river
at Eighth and Main.

All through the night I stare
at those persistent silent fires,
flames leaping like scarlet tongues.

AFTER THE FIRE

It was as if along with destruction
came the silencing of birds,
the grinding of the past into the mud.
Against blackened walls and solitary chimneys,
an awful quiet shrouded the city.

"Was it to this end we had fought and starved
and gone naked and cold,
husbandless and fatherless, our homes in ruins?"

    LADIES OF RICHMOND
    —Edited by Catherine Jones

XIX. THE BURIAL OF JOHN CRUMLEY,
April 10, 1865

On the day of Richmond's destruction
I lose John Crumley too—
our Irish gardener
who could coax vegetables from stones.
I think he died as much from sorrow
as infection of an old war wound,
his life finished with the war's end.
Now I feel like we've truly lost the war.

I fear he'll fall into Yankee hands
if I release his body.
I've kept him here a week
against all regulations.
Glad Betsy and I dress him
in worn shoes and a butternut uniform,
much too large, but clean. He would have
made a joke, and been pleased
at the bit of green ribbon Betsy
pins on him.
Tomorrow we will take him by cart
to Hollywood Cemetery
where he will rest
with countless brothers of the Cause.

ELEGY FOR JOHN

John Crumley rests by a willow tree
trundled there by Betsy and me,
far from his homeland by the sea.
He worked long hours for a minimum fee
with a gunshot wound in his good right knee.
Now he lies under a willow tree,
taken there by Betsy and me.

XX. CLOSING OF ROBERTSON'S, June 13, 1865

I have longed for this day,
and dreaded it too; curious to feel both ways.
I've accepted the fact
that Robertson's, like the war
is finished.

Thirteen hundred and thirty-three
came in rags and blood;
twelve hundred and sixty bodies healed,
if not their souls.

This morning I packed away
my reticule, my military commission.
I'll make the rounds once more
through these hollow halls,
devoid of nurses, patients, doctors.

So, close the door, turn the key,
leave the ghosts inside—
thank God, there are only seventy-three,
Will they wander and moan all night?
This is a heathen thought.

I cannot forget the past—
I can only walk away from it
on this bright June afternoon.

Stained glass window commemorating Sally Louisa Tompkins, St. James's Episcopal Church, Richmond, Virginia.

Photograph courtesy of St. James's Episcopal Church.

RICHMOND—1865-1916

Christ Church in Mathews, Virginia.

Photograph courtesy of
The Mathews County Historical Society.

I. FACING FACTS

What shall I do with myself
now the war is over? I wish I knew
worthwhile ways to spend the hours.
At thirty-two, my days stretch ahead,
terrifyingly empty.

For four years, head of Robertson's
I was accustomed to administer
to my men. Each day brimmed with problems,
ledgers to keep, decisions to be made.
Now retired, I'm only Sally Tompkins, spinster.

Through the terrible days and nights I prayed
for the maiming and the killing to cease.
Yet now I see my life revolved
around the horror of bloodshed, wounds and death,
Without war, I have no work.

"Physician, heal thyself."

II. ADJUSTING

The days pass pleasantly enough,
Sad Betsy cooks for me in our small house;
social gatherings at the Historical Society;
on Sunday afternoons I teach Bible class
in Saint James's Church.
The city begins to glow again
with fresh paint, new buildings,
Dogwood and azalea conceal
the scars of war.
If only my scars could be hidden under blossoms.
Spring doesn't come for me.
I can't sleep nights wondering
how former patients fare,
mourning those we lost.

I'm ashamed of my restlessness,
it nibbles at my days.
I volunteer to nurse
in a hospital for indigent ladies—
their ills so delicate, compared
to those of my brave boys;
the ragged wounds, sheets drenched in blood,
screams for morphine.
Oh, God, take my thoughts to calmer realms.
Did I grow too fond of fighting death?
No, God, but I grew accustomed to it.

III. TWO VERSIONS OF A JOURNEY TO
GLOUCESTER AND MATHEWS COUNTY,
OCTOBER 1865

The Journal of Miss Emmie Crump

October 10, 1865
This seems a fitting occasion to begin entries in my
birthday present from Mama—a pretty diary bound in
red Morocco leather.
Aunt and I think cousin Sally requires diversion, of late
she suffers with the vapors—if she could only put aside
her grand and terrible memories of the war. We
suggest a trip to Gloucester and Mathews where we have
many kinfolk. It infuriates us, but we need permission
from the damnyankees to travel eighty miles in our own dear
Virginia. They call us Federal District One. In this
book I'll refer to the Yankees as DY.

October 13, 1865
At last we're off, today the sky heavy with clouds.
The escort cavalry officer in charge seems polite
(I don't trust him.) He is sort of handsome, thick
yellow hair shiny as ripe wheat in the sun. I catch
him ogling me with his brown eyes. I ignore him.
Twenty mounted soldiers accompany us, I suppose to
protect us from bandits. Southerners don't scare easy
after what we've been through. Aunt, my best friend
Minnie and I are in one wagon, Captain Sally & cousins
Annie and Ella in the other. The wagons are what the
army used for ambulances in the war. I think longingly of
Papa's coach and four we owned before the war. It is a
dreary day, not even cheered by the Autumn colors.

Around twilight we reach the home of Judge Jeffries, Aunt's second cousin. Happily we leave our watch dog DY captain. So wonderful to be welcomed by our own kind—to share the horrors of our wartime experiences.

October 14, 1865
We leave at dawn to join our DY escorts. The sun is up, we're just underway when I'm horrified to miss my diamond ring Papa gave me for my 21st birthday. I could weep, but I'd bite my lips raw rather than display weakness in front of the DY. Then I remember where I left it, on the washstand at the Jeffries. The Captain says he cannot turn back, but offers to send one of his men for it. Absolutely not, I wouldn't dream of trusting my precious ring to a DY. Slow going today—the roads nothing better than trails, rutted and overgrown with weeds. We are sad, so much desolation—barns and houses burned, gardens trampled, fences broken down.

October 15, 1865
Our third evening, we arrive at Gloucester Courthouse. To our disgust, the DY soldiers stationed there are grossly inebriated. Papa always said only a true Southerner could hold his liquor. Too late and dark to press on to "Auburn," the captain and Aunt argue about where we should lodge. Cousin Sally, who has completely ignored all the DYs til now, takes charge, directs the wagons to the home of her friends the Taliferros. They welcomed us, and somehow fed and bedded us.

October 16, 1865
Our fourth day and we leave at first light—around eight
o'clock we arrive at "Auburn," on the North River. It
is pitifully run down, no hands left to help. Our Tabb
cousins greet us and for the first time in my life I witness
Cousin Sally weeping, when she embraces her kin. She
stayed at "Auburn" when she was a child.

Cousin Ellen feeds us a delicious breakfast—herring
roe scrambled with eggs and yellow spoon bread. She
does not invite the DY captain inside, has Tansy take him
a tray—she reports his anger at not being asked to come in
the house. Later after the whole company have departed,
we discover a vindictive message written on, (of all
strange places) Baby William's wooden wagon. He
expressed his anger and contempt for our lack of
hospitality. How could he expect entertainment in a
Virginia household where hearts were sore, fair lands
wasted all on account of such as he. I wish he hadn't
been quite so handsome and, except for his foolish note,
he seemed in every way a gentleman.

The Federal Escort Officer's Version

I, Benjamin Talbot, only recently sent to Richmond
as part of this grim Army of Occupation,
am delighted when chosen by my Colonel
to escort wagons traveling to Gloucester Court House.
I've had a bellyfull of this dull assignment—
listing the Reb's unceasing complaints
in my stuffy office.
I suppose these travelers are high-born Southerners,
they snub me at every opportunity.
Occasionally I catch the pretty young ladies
casting glances under lashes in my direction;
the older lady is knowledgeable about local roadways.
I consult with her frequently.
The plain, stern looking one dressed in black
is called "Captain,"
she looks neither right nor left, spends her time reading.
Given full responsibility for their safety
I do not like them out of my sight,
but they insist on quartering overnight
with friends and relations.

On the second morning the one called Emmie
informs me she is missing a ring,
believes it's left behind where they passed the night.
I offer to send a man to fetch it
but she'll have none of that.
I vow she thinks I'd reverse the whole caravan for her jewel.
She is distractingly pretty
with her tipped nose and golden curls.
On our last evening we arrive at Gloucester Court House,
to find the Federal brigade stationed there

celebrating pending departure with drinking and gambling;
makes me damned angry. I cannot leave these Rebs unattended.
The grim lady Miss Tompkins takes command,
decides where their party will pass the night,
I think she's a sour old maid,
but obviously accustomed to authority.

Next morning is fine, the sun warming North River.
Soon we arrive at a beautiful plantation,
the driveway planted with magnolia trees,
the house itself well proportioned,
though suffering from neglect.
My wagon load of women are greeted
with tears and joy by the owners.
I contemplate the role of Southern planter,
my foolish daydreaming rudely interrupted
when a housemaid thrusts a tray in my hands;
I'm startled then enraged
to be left under a tree with a tin plate
of cold cornbread and molasses.

Childish though it is, I feel insulted,
and cannot resist writing my sentiments
on a child's small wagon left outside.
I feel no malice toward these rebels,
I'm puzzled as to why they hold me in such low esteem.
I spent the war at Harvard,
after graduation joined a regiment
sent to occupy Richmond.
I've never harmed one Southerner.

Our mission accomplished,
there's nothing to do but leave.
As we ride down the magnolia-shaded lane,
I am overcome with longing
for New England spruce and hemlock,
and the sight of sun glinting off Narragansett Bay.

IV. SALLY KEEPS BUSY

One thing I forgot during the war
was how to amuse myself.
Ladies of my former staff
are back to giving tea parties.
(I'm still awed by the reappearance of tea.)
They reorganize cotillions,
in spite of a shortage of dancing partners.
Now that laudanum and morphine are available,
I'm distressed to learn of its misuse,
even though it's a balm for unhealed wounds.

I find travel a good pastime;
each month I seek a new destination.
I visit the Lightfoots at Port Royal,
old friends in Charlottesville,
Colonel Taylor's family in Norfolk.
It's pleasant to sail by packet boat
from Richmond to Williams Wharf in Mathews
where I stay at "Woodstock," home of my Lane cousins,
close by Poplar Grove.
The old house stands, the tide mill burned by Yankees,
the new one not yet finished.
Now there are new owners, I do not feel part of it;
I miss the beloved presence of Mama, Maria, Phoebe,
all gone before me. At Christ Church
I commune again with Lizzie,
but hurry back to the river, the marshes and reeds,
all blessedly the same.

In Richmond I believe I'm considered
something of an oddity—harmless, so I'm tolerated.
Coffee from the north
filters onto shelves of local grocers.
I will not drink Yankee coffee,
nor patronize merchants who sell it.
I admit to one eccentricity,
I cannot bring myself to buy Federal postage,
ask neighbor boys to do it for me,
and deliver my local mail by hand.
When confined at home I pass much time
maintaining a large correspondence
with my nieces and nephews;
I know it's my duty to nurture them
with scripture references, the best advice
in this bleak time of reconstruction.
Sometimes I read about others in my profession—
Florence Nightingale, Clara Barton and two writers
turned nurse, Louisa M. Alcott and Walt Whitman,
the latter most disturbing.

And so the weeks, even months go fast,
I only count from Sunday to Sunday.
I live neither in the future not the past,
the future too empty, the past too full.

V. THE GRAND REUNION, June 30-July 3, 1896

Our fair Richmond, queen city of the south
sparkles with flags, bunting, festoons of ribbon.
Five other reunions here
since the war ended,
but none this big nor so well attended.
Confederate colors brighten the summer sky.
High above them we're compelled
to raise the Union flag.
But this is a happy time; I intend to be happy,
fortunate I could rent the large dwelling
built on the same spot where once our hospital stood.

I extend invitations to all my boys,
provide private lodging for those who cannot
pay for hotel rooms; many bring families,
I feel that they all belong to me.
Above the door hangs a greeting,
"Welcome, Veterans of Robertson's Hospital;"
on our flagstaff fly our beloved stars and bars,
glorious, in spite of the Yankees' drooping colors.

I've dipped deep into my purse to provide
the most delicious viands available,
Smithfield hams from Surry, crab meat from the York River,
mounds of fried chicken, collards and potato salad,
custards, pudding, enough chocolate cakes
for all my boys, their wives and children.
For Auld Lang Syne we'll drink Confederate lemonade.

Forty generals in attendance,
among them Longstreet and Wade Hampton.
Mosby's men have gathered,
cadets from V.M.I. parade
with brave Choctaw Indian veterans.
Mrs. Jefferson Davis, widow of the President,
is here for the laying of the cornerstone
to the monument honoring her husband.
(He's still a hero in my eyes
for allowing Robertson's to remain open.)

In the back of my old hospital register
I'll paste the name cards given me
by my former patients,
In the dark winter ahead,
I'll think of this reunion,
the Confederate colors shimmering in the July heat
of Richmond, the thrilling notes of "DIXIE"—
like a final salute.

VI. EX-CORPORAL JENKIN'S OBSERVATIONS AT THE REUNION

I leave the wife and kids in Tennessee
to come to Richmond again,
I want Cpt. Tompkins to see
how a dirt-poor soldier changed
into a respectable married man.
Still the flesh pots beckon—
boat trips down to Norfolk
with pretty women on board;
there's vaudeville at the theaters,
gambling at the track.
But I've got to turn my back on these amusements.
Instead, dressed in my new checked suit, I drink lemonade
with Miss Sally, thank her for reading me Scripture,
and saving the soul of a poor country boy.

VI. (2) CAPTAIN ANTHONY SNOWDEN'S RESPONSE TO CAPTAIN TOMPKIN'S INVITATION

Dearest of captains, I deeply regret.
I cannot be there with you and your brave men;
pressing affairs keep me at home,
and unfortunately I'm rather in debt.
I'll never forget outwitting the Yanks.
It was great sport for me,
and a privilege to serve you.
God bless, dearest of captains.

VI. (3) WHY WILLIAM B. GRAVES ATTENDED

On the day the Yankees marched into Richmond
I was so bold as to ask permission
to enter Robertson's hospital,
with only a minor ankle sprain,
I was the last patient on the register,
number thirteen hundred and thirty-four.
The fame of Cpt. Sally Tompkins's hospital
was such that I wanted to be able to tell
children and grandchildren I was a patient there.
And now I've come to this reunion
to pay respects to the little lady
with healing in her milk-white hands.

VII. AT THE RICHMOND HOME FOR CONFEDERATE WOMEN (1906-1916)
3 East Grace Street, Richmond, Virginia

These four walls are my home now,
a retreat for the indigent, lonely and ill.
The ladies invite me to remain for my lifetime.
I politely refuse their charity,
insist that I pay.
It is a pleasant sanctuary;
I'm treated with great solicitude.

Sometimes residents bring treasures
from their trunks in the attic;
lace fans, silk ball gowns of a style long gone.
How we cling to these bits of another era.
Mrs. Fitzhugh Lee makes us weep
when she warbles "Somebody's Darling."
On holidays school children come to sing
"The Bonnie Blue Flag," recite "Little Griffin of Tennessee."
I welcome visitors from my past,
former patients, young doctors grown old and bearded;
Belle Stuart, a great grandmother, twice widowed,
now full blown and repetitious.

In the room next door lives General Pickett's niece,
whose hair hangs to her knees.
I've heard that as a child Marse Robert
patted her on the head;
she vowed she'd never cut the hair
touched by our saintly General.
Now Marse Robert's dead,
and she still has that long mane
(a nuisance to herself and others,)
We old ladies without men
have only memories left to nourish us.

VIII. EXCERPTS FROM CAPTAIN SALLY'S WILL,
April 15, 1907

I leave one hundred and fifty dollars each
to ten nephews, nieces and friends;
one thousand dollars to Richmond's Sheltering Arms Hospital
and to Christ Church in Mathews;
nine hundred dollars to Memorial Hospital, Richmond
(since I have already given them $100.)
To the Home for needy Confederate Women
(there are countless numbers of them)
I leave one thousand dollars.
To the Confederate Museum I bequeath
Robertson's Hospital register,
my officer's commission,
and the reticule.

I will Cousin Ellen my black silk skirt,
her sister Kate, my astrakhan cape;
for niece Ellen Wise I leave my sugar dish
and cream pot of solid silver.
As for my silver spoons I desire they be sold,
the money received used to purchase a *simple*
communion service for Christ Church.
To Cousin Hal Brooks I leave my gold watch
he's admired so long; I desire
that he obey the message engraved in its case:
"Redeem Time."

Heed this request, the most important of all:
that I be interred by Sister Elizabeth's grave
in the church yard under the pine and magnolia trees.
Then my life-long wish fulfilled,
that we lie side by side for eternity.

IX. SALLY DAYDREAMS

Now that I've committed my requests to paper,
I see fit to sit on the veranda,
and watch the setting sun,
relieved this job is finished.
At peace, I'll indulge myself in dreaming of the past;
usually I think my time can be better spent.

I drift back to Poplar Grove, when I was a girl,
to the Tide Mill and the river sounds,
the wind blowing through the reeds.
I think of people who have gone before me;
Mama, Phoebe, beloved brother and sisters.
I remember the woods,
laced with dogwood in the spring,
and the blue flight of the birds.
Like an old wound, I think of the war,
four years at Robertson's,
close to the comforting murmur of the James.
So many faces, names—
Judge Crump, John Crumley, Dr. Garnett,
Captain Snowden, the incorrigible Cpl. Jenkins.

I am ready, Lord.
Now evening birds settle into hydrangea bushes,
shadows begin to blot out the sun.

X. From THE RICHMOND TIMES-DISPATCH,
   July 26, 1916

"Captain Sally Louisa Tompkins, 83 years old, died yesterday of chronic nephritis at 8:45 o'clock in the morning, in the Home for Confederate Women. The funeral, with full military honors, will take place in Mathews County in the graveyard of the church which her sister, Miss Elizabeth Tompkins, helped to establish in 1841."

X. LOOKING FOR SALLY

The People:
      "Where can we find you, dearest of Captains?"

In Richmond on corner of Third and Main
a shiny bronze plaque
marks the site of Robertson's Hospital.
Search through the Confederate Museum,
next door to President Davis' home.
My reticule and register rest there
in a glass case.
Attend a service at Saint James's Church,
where a stained glass window memorializes me.
But you must look further still to find me.

I flow with the river by Poplar Grove,
with bluebirds I sweep down the slope,
below the house with white columns,
past the bulk of the new Tide Mill.

Down a small lane in a grove of trees,
find old Christ Church's graveyard.
There I sleep by my sister,
and there you can end your search.

"I was hungred and ye gave me meat,
I was thirsty and ye gave me drink,
I was sick and ye visited me."

XII. JOHN LENNON REMEMBERS

—On March 25, 1980 Pentacles Realty Inc., representing
John Lennon and Yoko Ono purchases Poplar Grove.

Didn't have it long, bought it for tax shelter,
didn't know what we were getting—
an old house by the river with a tide mill nearby;
no life around except rabbits, quail and deer,
saw some bluebirds once.

I heard how a girl named Sally
was born there,
grew up to be a nurse in the Yanks' Civil War;
how all the wounded chaps fell for her.
Yoko and I spent a night there,
I'd have gone barmy if we'd stayed any longer.
The only sounds were the wind blowing
through the poplar trees,
and the mournful sighs of the river.

ABOUT THE AUTHOR

Keppel Hagerman, a poet and fiction writer, was born in Richmond, Virginia and graduated from Duke University. During her husband's thirty year naval career, she and their three children lived in Germany, Paris, Washington, Norfolk and Seoul, Korea where she volunteered as an English teacher. Ms. Hagerman and her husband live in Charlottesville and Virginia Beach, Virginia. She is currently working on a volume of poetry and a collection of short stories.